HOCKEY TRIVIA for kids 2

Eric Zweig

Illustrations by
Lorna Bennett

Scholastic Canada Ltd.

Toronto New York London Auckland Sydney
Mexico City New Delhi Hong Kong Buenos Aires

Scholastic Canada Ltd.
604 King Street West, Toronto, Ontario M5V 1E1, Canada

Scholastic Inc.
557 Broadway, New York, NY 10012, USA

Scholastic Australia Pty Limited
PO Box 579, Gosford, NSW 2250, Australia

Scholastic New Zealand Limited
Private Bag 94407, Greenmount, Auckland, New Zealand

Scholastic Children's Books
Euston House, 24 Eversholt Street, London NW1 1DB, UK

To Amanda, who still likes baseball better.
— Eric

Photo credits:

Cover, p. 17, 21: Getty Images; p. 11: Imperial Oil-Turofsky/Hockey Hall of Fame; p. 35: Frank
Prazak/Hockey Hall of Fame; p. 46: Doug MacLellan/Hockey Hall of Fame; p. 49, 96 NHLI via
Getty Images; p. 73: Mike Bolt/Hockey Hall of Fame; p. 88: Portnoy/Hockey Hall of Fame; p. 95:
Miles Nadal/Hockey Hall of Fame

Library and Archives Canada Cataloguing in Publication

Zweig, Eric, 1963-

Hockey trivia for kids 2 / Eric Zweig.

ISBN 978-0-545-99699-0

1. Hockey--Miscellanea--Juvenile literature. 2. National Hockey

League--Miscellanea--Juvenile literature. I. Title.

GV847.25.Z943 2008   j796.962   C2008-901875-3

ISBN-10 0-545-99699-6

6 5 4 3 2 1   Printed in Canada   08 09 10 11 12

INTRODUCTION

Writing a book is hard work. In a book like this one, I try to remember the kinds of stories that interested me when I was a boy. Then I look for them: in newspapers, on the Internet, in hockey record books. I listen for good stories on television. There are lots of different places to find them. Collecting the information is fun. Getting it all organized is much harder.

When I wrote the first edition of *Hockey Trivia for Kids*, I thought I had done a pretty good job. Still, you never know for sure. The people at Scholastic seemed to like it too. That was a good sign. But it wouldn't matter if the kids it was written for didn't like it. Turns out, they did! I heard from lots of people who enjoyed the book . . . so I got the chance to write another one.

I still think the reason Canadians like hockey so much is because the game is so much fun. It's fun to play and it's fun to watch. It's even fun to read about! And even if most of us will never play in the NHL or at the Olympics — maybe even *because* we won't — there is still lots to enjoy about hockey our whole lives long.

Pick a Puck

Everyone knows that real hockey pucks are made of rubber. But if you're only playing hockey for fun, almost anything will do. Plastic pucks can be used for floor hockey; tennis balls work well for road hockey; even a tin of tuna works if you're playing on a frozen lake! But sometimes, people just have to get creative. This was especially true in hockey's early days. Back then a lump of coal may have been used as a puck. But it wasn't always the best idea, since it was pretty valuable and tended to break apart. A small bit of a sawed-off tree branch was better and cheaper. But there was another source of pucks that was absolutely free. Believe it or not, when horses used to pull carts on city streets, people often used their frozen plops of manure as hockey pucks. Yuck!

Fast Starters

Each year dozens of players make their debut in the NHL, although most of them see only limited action. Every so often, though, a rookie has such a spectacular season that it's obvious he's destined to become a real superstar. The 2005–06 season was unusual in that the NHL saw two incredible rookie performances.

Sidney Crosby was just 17 years old when he was chosen first overall by the Pittsburgh Penguins in the 2005 NHL Entry Draft. Two months after turning 18, he started his NHL career, getting two assists in his first two games. Then, in just his third game, he scored his first goal. It was a pretty good start to the season, and to his NHL career.

By the end of the 2005–06 season, Crosby had scored 39 goals and added 61 assists for a total of 102 points. He was the youngest player in NHL history to score 100 points in a season, and was just the seventh rookie in NHL history to do it. Still, Crosby wasn't even the top-scoring rookie in the NHL that season! That title belonged to Alexander Ovechkin, who also started off his NHL career with a bang.

Like Crosby, Ovechkin was also a number-one pick in the NHL Entry Draft — the Washington Capitals selected him first overall in 2004. Though he is two years older than Crosby, Ovechkin also made his NHL debut on October 5, 2005, due to the 2004–05 lockout. He didn't just score one goal in his very first game, he scored two!

Ovechkin's rookie season was even more spectacular than Crosby's. His 52 goals made him just the fourth rookie in NHL history to score 50 or more, and his 54 assists gave him 106 points.

Not bad for a couple of rookies!

Votes for Women

In December 2007 the International Ice Hockey Federation (IIHF) announced that three women had been voted into the IIHF Hall of Fame for the first time in its history. Angela James and Geraldine Heaney of Canada and Cammi Granato of the United States were officially inducted at a ceremony in May 2008.

CUP CHRONICLES

Luc Robitaille was a member of the Detroit Red Wings when he finally won the Stanley Cup in 2002. For most of his career Robitaille had starred with the Los Angeles Kings, so when he got to spend a day with the Stanley Cup, he brought it to Los Angeles. Robitaille loaded family and friends on a rented bus, and they all took the Cup on a tour of the city. His favourite stop was taking the Stanley Cup up to the famous Hollywood sign on the hillside above the city.

A Family Affair

Athletic skill seems to run in Alex Ovechkin's family. His father Mikhail was a professional soccer player in Russia. His mother Tatiana won Olympic gold medals in women's basketball in 1976 and 1980.

An Oldie but a Goodie

Fifty goals has long been a milestone in hockey. Most of the greatest scorers in NHL history have managed to top the 50-goal mark, but sometimes it takes a player a long time to get there. The NHL's oldest 50-goal scorer is John Bucyk. He was 35 years old when he scored 51 goals for the Boston Bruins in 1970–71. Teemu Selanne just missed breaking that record when he scored 48 goals in 2006–07 at the age of 36.

BY THE NUMBERS

Here's a look at the seven NHL rookies who have scored 100 points or more.

Player	*Team*
Teemu Selanne	Winnipeg Jets
Peter Stastny	Quebec Nordiques
Alex Ovechkin	Washington Capitals
Dale Hawerchuk	Winnipeg Jets
Joe Juneau	Boston Bruins
Sidney Crosby	Pittsburgh Penguins
Mario Lemieux	Pittsburgh Penguins

Year	Goals	Assists	Points
1992–93	76	56	132
1980–81	39	70	109
2005–06	52	54	106
1981–82	45	58	103
1992–93	32	70	102
2005–06	39	63	102
1984–85	43	57	100

Six of a Kind

The biggest hockey family in NHL history is the Sutter family of Viking, Alberta. Six Sutter boys played in the NHL, including twin brothers Rich and Ron. The other Sutters are Brent, Brian, Darryl and Duane.

Growing up on a farm in Alberta, the Sutters all pushed each other in everything they did, especially hockey. They weren't the most talented players, but they worked hard. Gary was the oldest of the boys, and the best according to his six brothers, but he left hockey early to help run the farm. Gary watched as Brian led the way to the NHL, paving a path for his five other siblings.

Brian, the eldest of the six Sutters who played in the NHL, was drafted by the St. Louis Blues in 1976 and began his NHL career the following year.

In terms of statistics, Brent was the most successful of the Sutter brothers. He played in 1,111 games and scored 363 goals. If you measure success by Stanley Cup wins, then Duane was the best. He won the Cup four times in a row with the New York Islanders in the early 1980s. Brother Brent played alongside him on two of those teams.

DID YOU KNOW?

Willie O'Ree became the first black player in NHL history when he played two games with the Boston Bruins in January of 1958. He also played 43 games with the Bruins during the 1960–61 season. Though his NHL career was brief, O'Ree had a very long career in professional hockey. It stretched from 1955 to 1979. From 1961–62 to 1973–74, O'Ree was one of the best — and most popular — players in the Western Hockey League, a top minor league. Almost nobody knew it during his playing days, but something made Willie O'Ree's career even more remarkable: he was almost completely blind in one eye. A puck struck O'Ree in his right eye during a game in the 1955–56 season. He lost 95 percent of his vision in that eye, and doctors told him he would never play hockey again. Proving them wrong, he returned to action just eight weeks later. Long after his playing career, Willie O'Ree was named Director of Youth Development for the NHL/USA Hockey Diversity Task Force in 1998.

Willie O'Ree

His First Wasn't First

Patrick Kane was the first player selected in the 2007 NHL Entry Draft. He played his first NHL game with the Chicago Blackhawks just a few months after that, on October 4, 2007, and he scored his first goal in his second game two days later . . . Or did he?

Kane scored the only goal in a shootout to give Chicago a 4–3 win over the Detroit Red Wings on October 6, 2007. However, goals scored in a shootout don't count as official goals in NHL statistics. So, even though he won the game for Chicago that night, Kane wasn't actually credited with scoring a goal! His first official goal came nearly two weeks later when he scored against the Colorado Avalanche on October 19.

CUP CHRONICLES

In February 2000, the Stanley Cup attended the Native Hockey Tournament at Rankin Inlet, Nunavut. The temperature was about −65 degrees Celsius! Still, some people drove nearly 400 kilometres on snowmobiles just to see the Cup. While it was there, the Cup toured the town and even made a brief stop inside an igloo.

Rules and Records

Wayne Gretzky holds a lot of NHL records, but because of some league rules, there are a couple he hasn't been able to lay claim to.

Gretzky had an incredible start to his NHL career. He had 137 points during his first NHL season in 1979–80. However, he didn't win the Calder Memorial Trophy, which goes to the rookie of the year. Why not? The NHL didn't consider Gretzky to be a rookie: he had spent the year before playing in the World Hockey Association (WHA), a rival professional hockey league.

Another league rule kept Gretzky from being the youngest player in history to win the Art Ross Trophy as the NHL scoring leader. Gretzky's 137 points in 1979–80 actually tied him for the league lead with NHL veteran Marcel Dionne. But because of a league rule that says if there's a tie for points in the Art Ross race, the trophy goes to the player who has scored the most goals that season, Dionne won it. He had had 53 goals; Gretzky had 51.

Gretzky won the Art Ross Trophy the following year, when he was 20. Sidney Crosby was 19 when he won the Art Ross Trophy in 2006–07, making him the youngest person in NHL history to win it.

DID YOU KNOW?

When Wayne Gretzky started playing hockey, he wore number 9 in honour of Gordie Howe, his favourite player. He didn't start wearing 99 until he played junior hockey with the Sault Ste. Marie Greyhounds. Another player already had 9, so Gretzky had to choose another one. He tried 14 and 19 before finally settling on 99.

DID YOU KNOW?

The NHL scoring race has ended in a tie two other times. Bobby Hull and Andy Bathgate both had 84 points in 1961–62. Hull won the Art Ross Trophy that year because he had 50 goals and Bathgate had only 28. Jaromir Jagr and Eric Lindros were tied for the league lead with 70 points in 1994–95. Jagr won the Art Ross Trophy that year because he had 32 goals and Lindros had 29.

Captain Kid

When the Pittsburgh Penguins named Sidney
Crosby their captain on May 31, 2007, he became
the youngest captain in NHL history. Crosby was
19 years and nine months old. Before Crosby,
Vincent Lecavalier was the youngest captain; he
was just 19 years and 10 months old when he was
named captain of the Tampa Bay Lightning late in
the 1999–2000 season.

Sidney Crosby at his first game as captain, October 5, 2008

Other 99s

Early in Wayne Gretzky's career, two other NHL players wore number 99. Wilf Paiement wore it for the Toronto Maple Leafs from 1979 to 1982, and Rick Dudley wore 99 for the Winnipeg Jets in 1980–81. Way back in 1934–35, three different players — Leo Bourgeault, Desse Roche, and Joe Lamb — wore 99 for the Montreal Canadiens, all in the same season!

Fast Tricks

The fastest hat trick in NHL history was scored in just 21 seconds. Bill Mosienko of the Chicago Black Hawks got three goals against the New York Rangers at 6:09, 6:20 and 6:30 of the third period on March 23, 1952. Mosienko's hat trick helped the Black Hawks rally to a 7–6 victory.

Almost 55 years later, on February 19, 2007, Ryan Malone of the Pittsburgh Penguins got his own unique kind of fast hat trick. Malone scored each of his three goals during the first minute of play in each period. He scored 45 seconds into the first period, 49 seconds into the second and 48 seconds into the third.

DID YOU KNOW?

The NHL changed its rule about minor penalties before the 1956–57 season. Until then, two-minute penalties lasted the full two minutes no matter how many goals were scored. The new rule allowed the penalized player to return to the ice if the team gave up a power-play goal.

The reason for the rule? The Montreal Canadiens' power-play was just too good! Take a look at the November 5th, 1955, game between the Boston Bruins and the Montreal Canadiens: Montreal's Jean Beliveau scored three goals against the Boston Bruins in just 44 seconds while the Canadiens had a man advantage. Ouch!

Rocketing to the Top

In 2006–07 Vincent Lecavalier became the first French-Canadian player to win the Maurice "Rocket" Richard Trophy, which was donated to the NHL by the Montreal Canadiens in 1999. The trophy is awarded each year to the player who leads the NHL in goals scored. Richard was a star player with the Canadiens from 1942 to 1960 and is a legendary hero in Quebec. He was the first player to score 50 goals in a season and the first to score 500 in his career.

Vincent Lecavalier receiving the Maurice Richard Trophy with The Rocket's brother, Henri

CUP CHRONICLES

Mark Messier is the only player in NHL history to captain two different Stanley Cup-winning teams. Messier was captain of the Edmonton Oilers when they won the Stanley Cup in 1990 and was also captain of the New York Rangers when they won in 1994.

You Say it's Your Birthday

Players like Sidney Crosby, Vincent Lecavalier, Patrick Kane and Wayne Gretzky are among many who have made it to the NHL at the age of 18. But can you imagine a hockey player making it to the NHL before he'd celebrated five birthdays? How about making the Hall of Fame before his 11th birthday? Impossible? Well, it's happened . . . sort of.

Henri Richard was born on February 29, 1936

— a leap day. Technically, his birthday comes around only once every four years. So when Maurice Richard's little brother reached the NHL in 1955, he'd only had four actual birthdays . . . even though he was really 19 years old. Henri Richard was 43 years old when he was inducted into the Hall of Fame in 1979 . . . but he wouldn't actually have his 11th birthday until one year later.

BY THE NUMBERS

Red Kelly won the Stanley Cup four times with the Detroit Red Wings in the 1950s and another four times with the Toronto Maple Leafs in the 1960s. He's the only person on the list of players with the most Stanley Cup championships who didn't win any his with the Montreal Canadiens. Here's the list of players with the most Cup wins:

Player	Cups
Henri Richard.	11
Jean Beliveau	10
Yvan Cournoyer.	10
Claude Provost	9
Red Kelly.	8
Maurice Richard.	8
Jacques Lemaire	8
Serge Savard.	7
Jean-Guy Talbot.	7

NAME GAME

The Carolina Hurricanes actually started out as the New England Whalers in the 1979–80 season in the World Hockey Association. "Whalers" was chosen for two reasons: it contains the letters of the league (WHA), and whaling had once been important part of Boston's history. So, when the team entered the NHL in 1979–80, it became known as the Hartford Whalers. In 1997 the Whalers moved from Hartford to Raleigh, North Carolina. The name then changed to Hurricanes because of the powerful storms that often hit the area.

DID YOU KNOW?

Fred Sasakamoose is recognized as the first Native person to play in the NHL. He played 11 games with the Chicago Black Hawks in 1953–54, making his debut at Maple Leaf Gardens in Toronto on February 27, 1954. A Cree, Sasakamoose was born on the Sandy Lake Reserve in Saskatchewan on December 25, 1933. He was inducted into the Saskatchewan Sports Hall of Fame in 2007.

However, some believe that Saskamoose may not really have been the first. Paul Jacobs, a Mohawk from Kahnawake, Quebec, went to training camp with the Toronto Arenas in 1918, but it's unclear if he ever actually played in a game. Others believe that Bud Maracle, who played 11 games for the

New York Rangers in 1930–31, may also have been Native. It's even possible that the old Springfield Indians minor league hockey team got its name because Maracle was one of the team's original players.

NAME GAME

Before moving to Arizona, the Phoenix Coyotes had been the Winnipeg Jets. The Jets' name started with a junior team in Winnipeg. Ben Hatskin, who ran the team, was a friend and admirer of the man who owned the New York Jets in the National Football League. The name followed Winnipeg into the World Hockey Association, then into the NHL. When the Jets moved to Phoenix in 1996, the name Coyotes was chosen in a name-the-team contest. Coyotes are common in the Arizona desert.

BY THE NUMBERS

Only five players in NHL history have had their numbers retired by two different teams.

Player	Number	Teams retired
Gordie Howe	9	Detroit Red Wings
		Hartford Whalers/
		Carolina Hurricanes
Bobby Hull	9	Chicago Blackhawks
		Winnipeg Jets/
		Phoenix Coyotes
Raymond Bourque	77	Boston Bruins
		Colorado Avalanche
Mark Messier	11	Edmonton Oilers
		New York Rangers
Wayne Gretzky	99	Edmonton Oilers
		New York Rangers

Empty Cup

In the spring of 2006, the Carolina Hurricanes beat the Edmonton Oilers to win the Stanley Cup. One year later, neither team even made it to the playoffs! That marked the first time since the NHL took control of the Cup in 1926–27 that both finalists from the year before failed to make the playoffs the next season.

NAME GAME

When the NHL added a new team in New York for the 1972–73 season, the name Islanders was chosen. It was picked because the team was based in Nassau County, on Long Island in the New York suburbs.

CUP CHRONICLES

When the New York Rangers won the Stanley Cup in 1994, it had been 54 years since the team's last win in 1940. To celebrate, Rangers players took the Cup all over the city. Some even said that Ed Olczyk took the Stanley Cup to the Belmont race track and let Kentucky Derby winner Go For Gin eat out of the bowl! Although Olczyk is a big horseracing fan, and admits he took the Cup to the track, he says that no horse ever ate out of it while the Cup was with him.

DID YOU KNOW?

When rookie Guillaume Latendresse wore 84 for the Montreal Canadiens in 2006–07, it meant that at some point in history a player in an NHL game had worn every number from 0 and 00 to 99.

First to 500

With a goal on October 19, 1957, Maurice "The Rocket" Richard of the Montreal Canadiens became the first player in NHL history to score 500 career goals. When Richard retired a few years later, he had scored 544 goals. Today, Wayne Gretzky holds the NHL career record with 894 goals. Still, the 500-goal plateau is considered a major milestone for any player who reaches it.

Three of a Kind

Before he reached the NHL, future Hall of Famer
Denis Savard was already part of a famous line
with the Montreal Junior Canadiens. Savard
centred Denis Cyr and Denis Tremblay on a line
known as "Les Trois Denis." Not only were all three
players named Denis, they had all been born on the
same day — February 4, 1961 — and they all
grew up within three blocks of each other in the
Montreal suburb of Verdun!

Doing it the Hard Way

Seven players in NHL history have entered the 500-goal club by scoring a hat trick to reach the milestone. The first was Jean Beliveau in 1971. The others are Wayne Gretzky, Mario Lemieux, Mark Messier, Brett Hull, Jaromir Jagr and Mats Sundin.

Fast Starter

Jordan Staal was the youngest player in the NHL during his rookie season of 2006–07. He turned 18 only a few weeks before the season began. On October 21, 2006, he became the youngest player in NHL history to score a goal on a penalty shot. On February 10, 2007, he became the youngest player ever to score a hat trick.

One is the Loneliest Number

Until the 1960s, every NHL team only had one goalie on its roster. In the early days, if a goalie got hurt in a game, play was delayed until he could be patched up. If the goalie was hurt too badly to continue, his team would actually have to put another player in net!

In 1950 the NHL passed a new rule that said every home team had to have a spare goalie at each game. This goalie would take over for either team in case of an injury or illness. These so-called "house goalies" were usually the team trainer, or a local amateur star. The most famous house goalie was Ross "Lefty" Wilson. Wilson was a former minor league goalie who served as the Detroit Red Wings' assistant trainer and often went in net during practice. Three times between 1953 and 1957, Wilson had to take over in goal during games played at the Detroit Olympia. In all, Wilson played a total of 85 minutes and only allowed one goal!

Number Four, Bobby Orr

Bobby Orr wore number 4 when he starred with the Boston Bruins in the 1960s and '70s. His name and the number just seem to go together — maybe because they rhyme! But Orr was given a different number when he first joined the Bruins. He wore 30 when he got to his first training camp, and wore 27 in exhibition games. At the time, Albert "Junior" Langois wore 4 for Boston. When Langois got injured, then sent to the minors, Orr asked if he could have Langois' number. Orr had worn 2 when he played junior hockey, but Boston had retired that number in honour of another great defenseman, Eddie Shore. The Bruins had also retired 3, so Orr figured 4 was as close as he could get!

Bobby Orr, wearing number 27, with Harry Sinden

They Don't Ask How, Just How Many

It wasn't pretty when Jeremy Roenick scored his 500th career goal for the San Jose Sharks on November 17, 2007. Roenick dumped the puck into the Phoenix Coyotes end from outside the blue line. The puck hit the glass behind the net, bounced off the goal, deflected off goalie Alex Auld's skate, twirled toward the goal line and then skittered in off of Auld's stick. "I wish for his sake it could have been nicer," Auld said.

DID YOU KNOW?

Lanny McDonald is the only player in NHL history to score exactly 500 goals during his career. The Calgary Flames star scored his 500th goal, got his 1,000th point and won the Stanley Cup for the first time all in his final NHL season of 1988–89.

The Champion of Champions

Henri Richard has more Stanley Cup rings than fingers! Richard played on more Stanley Cup-winning teams than any player in hockey history. He played with the Montreal Canadiens for 20 seasons (1955–56 to 1974–75) and won the Stanley Cup 11 times. Jean Beliveau nearly matched Richard's record, playing on 10 Stanley Cup-winning teams during his 20 seasons in Montreal. But he has his name engraved on the Stanley Cup 17 times. Why? After his playing career, Beliveau was part of seven more championship teams while working in the Canadiens' front office.

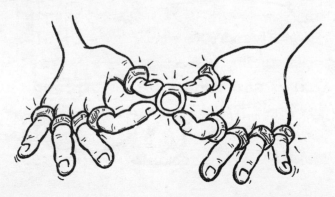

DID YOU KNOW?

The tradition of naming three stars at a hockey game goes back to the 1936–37 season. That year Imperial Oil became the main sponsor of Hockey Night in Canada *broadcasts on the radio*. Imperial Oil came up with the idea of naming three stars as a way to promote its "3 Star" brand of gasoline at Esso stations.

Gretzky's Little Brother

Wayne Gretzky has a brother who also played in the NHL. Brent Gretzky played in 10 games for the Tampa Bay Lightning in 1993–94. He played in three games with Tampa the following year before being sent back to the minors. Brent Gretzky scored just one goal in his NHL career.

NAME GAME

When Pittsburgh got an NHL expansion team in 1967, the name Penguins was the winner of a contest to give the team an identifying symbol.

BY THE NUMBERS

Joe Malone was one of the greatest goal scorers in early hockey history. On January 31, 1920, Malone scored seven goals in a single game! That's an NHL record that still stands. Over the years, seven different players (including Joe Malone himself) have come close to the record by scoring six goals in a game. Here are those players:

Player	Team
Newsy Lalonde	Montreal Canadiens
Joe Malone	Quebec Bulldogs
Corb Denneny	Toronto St. Pats
*Cy Denneny	Ottawa Senators
Syd Howe	Detroit Red Wings
Red Berenson	St. Louis Blues
Darryl Sittler	Toronto Maple Leafs

*Corb Denneny and Cy Denneny were brothers.

Date

January 10, 1920

March 10, 1920

January 26, 1921

March 7, 1921

February 3, 1944

November 7, 1968

February 7, 1976

In 1964 an injury to goalie Terry Sawchuk forced the Detroit Wings to use minor leaguer Bob Champoux in a playoff game. Even though the Red Wings won 5–4, the NHL decided this wasn't a fair way to do things. A new rule was introduced saying that every team would have to have two goalies dressed for playoff games in 1965. Then, before the start of the 1965–66 season, the rule was expanded to say that every team had to have two goalies in their lineup for every single NHL game.

That's Gotta Hurt!

When Bobby Hull starred in the 1960s, he had the hardest shot in the NHL. He may even have had the hardest shot of all time: measuring devices weren't as accurate then, but it was said he could shoot the puck 193 kilometres per hour!

Going in Goal

The first player to take over in goal during an NHL game was a defenseman named Harry Mummery. In a game against the Ottawa Senators on February 4, 1920, Quebec Bulldogs goalie Frank Brophy was struck by a hard shot right over his heart. There were only two minutes left in the second period, but Brophy couldn't continue, so veteran Mummery took over and stayed in net for the rest of the game. He was bombarded with more than 30 shots but only let in three. Still, Ottawa beat Quebec 5–0. Later in the season, Quebec used Mummery in goal again for two full games, both of which were also against the Senators. On March 8, Mummery was beaten for 11 goals in an 11–4 loss, but just two days later, Mummery and the Bulldogs beat Ottawa 10–4.

Mummery made one final appearance as a goalie during the 1921–22 season, once again against Ottawa. But this time Mummery was playing for the Hamilton Tigers. Hamilton goalie Howard Lockhart was hit in the face by a shot (goalies didn't wear masks at the time) near the end of the first period. It was 4–1 for Ottawa when Mummery took over, but he allowed the Senators just two more goals and Hamilton rallied to win 7–6 in overtime.

Think They Needed a Rest?

The NHL record for most goals in a single period is nine. The Buffalo Sabres scored nine times against the Toronto Maple Leafs in the second period of a game on March 19, 1981. The final score that night was 14–4.

Like Father,
Like Son

Bobby Hull and Brett Hull are the only father-son combination in hockey history to have both scored over 500 goals in their careers. Bobby scored 610 goals in his NHL career; Brett scored 741.

Brett Hull accepting the Hart Trophy with father Bobby.

Howe Could He Compete?

When it comes to NHL families, Gordie Howe is most famous for playing alongside his two sons, Mark and Marty. But did you know that Gordie Howe also had a brother who played in the NHL? Vic Howe didn't do quite as well as his older sibling. He played for the New York Rangers, but he only played in 33 games during parts of three seasons in the 1950s. Gordie Howe scored 801 goals in his NHL career; Vic Howe only scored 3.

That One Was Easy

Three of hockey's greatest goal scorers scored their 500th career goal into an empty net: Mike Bossy, Wayne Gretzky and Jari Kurri.

Goals and Saves

Toronto Maple Leafs star Charlie Conacher was the NHL's top goal scorer five times in six seasons between 1930–31 and 1935–36. But his talents weren't limited to just scoring: Conacher was pretty good at preventing goals too! He took over in net four times in his career when his goalie was either injured or penalized. He played a total of 10 minutes in the net during his career and never gave up a single goal.

Bobby's Brother

Bobby Hull not only had a star hockey player for a son, he had a brother who was pretty good too. Dennis Hull played in the NHL for 14 seasons from 1964 to 1978. He and Bobby were teammates with the Chicago Black Hawks for eight seasons. Dennis scored 40 goals in his best season in 1970–71, and had 303 in his career. Combined with Bobby's 610 goals, that gives the Hulls 913. No two brothers in NHL history have ever scored more.

Classy Cassie

On October 14, 2006, Cassie Campbell became the first woman to do colour commentary on a *Hockey Night in Canada* broadcast. A year later, in the fall of 2007, she became the first women's hockey player to be inducted into Canada's Sports Hall of Fame. Cassie Campbell retired as a player in 2006 after playing as a top forward and captaining the Canadian Olympic women's hockey team in 2002 and 2006.

Cassie Campbell behind the *Hockey Night in Canada* desk

DID YOU KNOW?

Maurice Richard, Gordie Howe and Bobby Hull all famously wore number 9 on their sweaters. However, none of them started off with that number. Richard actually wore 15 when he joined the Montreal Canadiens, but asked to switch to 9 when his first child was born and weighed 9 pounds (4 kilograms). Howe wore 17 when he first joined the Detroit Red Wings, but asked to switch to 9 after he figured out that players with lower numbers got better seats when the team travelled by train. Hull wore 16, then 7, before he finally settled on 9.

CUP CHRONICLES

King Clancy is the only player to play all six positions in a single Stanley Cup game. He did it with the Ottawa Senators on March 31, 1923. Clancy faced off as a centre, played both sides of the defense and skated up and down both wings too. Then, when Ottawa goalie Clint Benedict was penalized for slashing, Clancy took a two-minute turn between the pipes.

DID YOU KNOW?

On December 21, 1937, Paul Thompson of the Chicago Black Hawks slapped a shot past Boston Bruins goalie Cecil "Tiny" Thompson. This was the first time in NHL history that a player scored a goal against his brother. Paul scored with just nine seconds left in the game to break his older brother's shutout, but Tiny held on for a 2–1 victory.

Penalties Too

Injuries weren't the only reason players sometimes had to take over in goal. In the early days of the NHL, goalies actually had to serve their own penalties. When a goalie was sent to the penalty box, his team had to scramble to find a player to replace him. In those days a minor penalty lasted a full two minutes, even if a team scored a power-play goal, so a penalty to a goalie could mean real trouble.

A game between the Boston Bruins and the Toronto Maple Leafs on March 15, 1932, is a perfect example of how bad things could get for a team if they lost their goalie to a penalty. Maple Leafs goalie Lorne Chabot was called for tripping early in the first period. The Leafs tried using three different defensemen in the net, but the Bruins scored a goal against each one of them! Boston went on to win the game 6–2.

Lester to the Rescue

The most famous case of a non-goalie guarding the net in an NHL game came during the 1928 Stanley Cup Finals. But it wasn't a player who took over this time: it was the coach.

The New York Rangers had already lost the first game to the Montreal Maroons. Now, midway through the second period of the game, it was scoreless. Then a shot struck the Rangers' goalie, Lorne Chabot, directly on his left eye. He couldn't continue and was sent to the hospital.

The Rangers had no spare goalie. Alec Connell of the Ottawa Senators was at the game in Montreal that night, so the Rangers asked for permission to borrow him. The Maroons said no. The players insisted that the Rangers had to follow the rules about using someone who was already on their team. Coach Lester Patrick chose himself.

Patrick had once been a star defenseman. He'd played a full season as recently as 1925–26, and he had once played 10 minutes in goal back in

1921–22. Still, he was now 44 years old. Could he possibly hold back the Maroons' powerful attack?

With the Rangers playing tight defense in front of him, Patrick stopped every shot he faced but one. The Rangers managed one goal themselves, so the game went into overtime. Then, at 7:05 of the extra session, the Rangers scored again. Even the Maroons fans stood and cheered as Lester led the Rangers off the ice.

After the game the Maroons agreed to let the Rangers use Joe Miller of the New York Americans for the rest of the series. Following a 2–0 loss to the Maroons in game three, Miller posted a shutout of his own in game four to push the best-of-five series to the limit. Miller was cut and suffered two black eyes in game five, but he hung on for a 2–1 victory that gave the Rangers the Stanley Cup.

DID YOU KNOW?

Two or more teammates have each scored 50 goals in the same season 25 times in NHL history, but only one pair of teammates has scored its 50th goals in the same game. Mario Lemeiux and Kevin Stevens both got their 50th goals for the Pittsburgh Penguins on March 21, 1993.

Made to Measure

In the earliest days of hockey, goalies didn't wear much more protection than any other player. Then, in the early 1890s, goalies began wearing cricket pads on their legs. The pads helped to ease the pain from hard shots, but since they wrapped so closely around a goalie's legs, the puck sometimes would deflect off them and keep on going right into the net.

In the 1920s, special pads — much wider than cricket pads — began to be made especially for hockey goalies. In order to make sure that goalies didn't wear pads that were so wide they blocked too much of the net, the NHL passed a rule before the 1925–26 season that said goalie pads could not be more than 12 inches (30 centimetres) wide. Over the years, the rule flip-flopped between 12 inches, 10 inches (25 centimetres) and 12 inches again. Then another change was made following the 2004–2005 lockout, when the NHL introduced several new rules in order to bring more scoring back in the game. Now goalie pads cannot be more than 11 inches (28 centimetres) wide.

Pop's Pads

Emil (Pop) Kenesky made harnesses for horses in Hamilton, Ontario. By 1917, he had opened his own business. But Pop was also a hockey fan. While watching local church league games in the early 1920s, he noticed the way shots sometimes bounced into the net right off a goalie's cricket pads, and he didn't like it. Using the tools of his harness-making trade, Pop began making improvements to the pads the local goalies were wearing.

Percy Thompson was the owner of the Hamilton Tigers NHL team. In 1924 he asked Pop to repair the pads of Tigers goalie Jake Forbes. The Tigers had always been a bad team, but once Forbes started wearing his new Kenesky pads, the team started to win. Soon, other NHL goalies were asking Pop to make pads for them too.

Pop Kenesky's pads were made of leather and stuffed with deer hair and kapok (a silky fibre made from the seeds of tropical plants). All the pads were handmade, so it took a long time to make them. He could never make very many at a time, but all the best goalies in hockey wanted to use Kenesky pads. So Pop just kept on making them. He put in a full eight hours a day at his store until he was 86 years old.

Kenesky pads remained very popular in the NHL right up until the 1990s. By then, new materials had become available. Pads could now be made much more quickly, and they were much lighter and stayed drier too. There is still a Kenesky Sports store in Hamilton, and it still sells goalie equipment, but the store is no longer owned by the Kenesky family and it no longer makes its own brand of equipment.

DID YOU KNOW?

Of all the fathers and sons who have played in the NHL, Bobby Hull and Brett Hull are the only ones who have both won the Hart Trophy as league MVP. Bobby won the Hart Trophy in 1965 and 1966. Brett won it 1991.

All Hail Hayley

In December 2007, Hayley Wickenheiser became the first hockey player ever to be named Canada's female athlete of the year. Wickenheiser took over from Cassie Campbell as captain of the national women's hockey team in 2007 and led Canada in reclaiming the World Championship from the United States. She had eight goals and six assists in five games at the tournament and was named the most valuable player.

DID YOU KNOW?

Wayne Gretzky, Jari Kurri and Glenn Anderson are the only three teammates to each score 50 goals in the same season, and they did it twice! All three topped 50 with the Edmonton Oilers in 1983–84 and 1985–86.

NAME GAME

San Jose joined the NHL for the 1991–92 season. Like many team names, the name Sharks was picked out of 5,000 entries in a name-the-team contest. There are many shark research facilities in the San Francisco Bay area in California, where San Jose is located.

He Shoots – He Scores!!

Last of His Kind

On October 16, 1960, Jerry Toppazzini of the Boston Bruins became the last position player to play goal in an NHL game. At the time, no player had been forced to replace a goalie since 1941. But Boston goalie Don Simmons was cut under the eye by a shot from Chicago Black Hawks' Eric Nesterenko with less than 30 seconds remaining in the game. Rather than wait for the Black Hawks' house goalie to suit up, Toppazzini went in the net instead. He didn't face any shots as the final few seconds wound down.

NAME GAME

When Chicago entered the NHL in 1926, owner Frederic McLaughlin chose the name Blackhawks for his team. McLaughlin had served in the United States army during World War I as a member of the 86th Division, which was known as the Black Hawk Division. (The Black Hawk Indians used to live in the area where many of the 86th Division soldiers came from.) Until the 1984–85 NHL season, the name Chicago Blackhawks was usually written as two words, "Black Hawks."

DID YOU KNOW?

The first goalie to actually score a goal by shooting the puck the length of the ice into an open net was Ron Hextall of the Philadelphia Flyers. Hextall scored after the Boston Bruins pulled their goalie in a game on December 8, 1987. To prove it was no fluke, he did it again in a playoff game against the Washington Capitals two years later. Since then, several other goalies have scored goals too. Some, like Hextall, have shot the puck in, but others, like Billy Smith, were simply the last player on their team to touch the puck before someone else scored in their own net.

CUP CHRONICLES

Hal Winkler's name appears on the Stanley Cup with the 1929 Boston Bruins even though he didn't play a single minute with the team that season! Winkler had starred for Boston in 1927–28, but was in the minors in 1928–29. Still, his name got engraved on the Stanley Cup as the Bruins' "sub-goaltender."

65

Thanks for Coming

Goalie Robbie Irons was just expecting to sit on the bench when he was called up to the St. Louis Blues for a game on November 13, 1968. After all, the Blues had two future Hall of Fame goaltenders on their roster: Jacques Plante was out with a groin injury, but that still left Glenn Hall to play. Unfortunately for the Blues, Hall got into an argument with the referee just two minutes after the opening face-off that night and was given a game misconduct.

Blues coach Scotty Bowman didn't think that Irons was ready to play. He told his rookie goalie to stall for time while Plante came down from the stands to suit up. But the referee wasn't buying Irons' stall tactics. Faced with a two-minute delay-of-game penalty, Bowman sent Irons into the net. By 5:01 of the first period, Plante was ready. Irons had played just three minutes (and faced no shots), but his moment in the spotlight was over. He played 12 more years in the minor leagues, but never got another chance in the NHL.

DID YOU KNOW?

On March 31, 1994, Christian Soucy played three minutes in goal for the Chicago Blackhawks. It was the only NHL appearance of his career, so Soucy and Robbie Irons are considered tied for the shortest careers in NHL history. However, Soucy actually played three minutes and 21 seconds, while Irons only played three minutes and one second.

Bep Was Just a Boy

The youngest player in NHL history was Armand "Bep" Guidolin. Bep Guidolin was just 16 years old when he joined the Boston Bruins in 1942–43. With so many older hockey players serving in the military during World War II, many young players got an early chance to play in the NHL.

The Boston Bruins posted a record of 38–5–1 during a 44-game season in 1929–30. In today's 82-game NHL, that would equal a record of 70–10–2 and 144 points! The Bruins never lost two games in a row during the entire season . . . until they reached the Stanley Cup Final. Then the Montreal Canadiens swept Boston for two straight wins in a best-of-three series. After that, the NHL expanded the Finals to a best-of-five series. The current best-of-seven playoff format was introduced in 1939.

NAME GAME

St. Louis, Missouri, is well-known for a type of music called "the blues." There was even a popular song around 1917 called "The St. Louis Blues," written by W.C. Handy, who is often referred to as "the Father of the Blues." It seemed only fitting that the hockey team take the name the St. Louis Blues.

Working Overtime

The Toronto Maple Leafs and Boston Bruins were the two best teams in the NHL during the 1932–33 season. It was not surprising that their semifinal playoff series that year was a close one. In fact, the first three games of the best-of-five series each went into overtime. The fifth and final game was played on April 3, 1933. It went into overtime too.

Boston and Toronto played three gruelling 20-minute overtime periods that night. That's like playing another full hockey game! Still nobody scored. Finally, in the fourth extra period, Toronto's King Clancy put the puck past Boston goalie Tiny Thompson — but a whistle had sounded just before Clancy shot. No goal.

After a fifth scoreless overtime session, NHL president Frank Calder said the teams should toss a coin to decide the winner. Another suggestion was to continue the game without any goalies. The players on both teams were exhausted, but they decided to play on until somebody won the game fair and square.

Finally, four-and-a-half minutes into the sixth overtime period, Maple Leafs forward Ken Doraty took a pass from Andy Blair. He went wide around the Boston defense and scored! Toronto won the game 1–0 after 104 minutes and 46 seconds of overtime.

Only one game in NHL history has ever lasted longer than the Toronto-Boston playoff game in 1933. In 1936, the Montreal Maroons beat the Detroit Red Wings in a game that lasted 116 minutes and 30 seconds of overtime.

DID YOU KNOW?

To get your name on the Stanley Cup today, you have to play at least 40 regular-season games or one game in the playoff Finals. If a player falls short of that, his team may ask the NHL for permission to include his name on the Cup.

No Ordinary Joe

Joe Thornton was the first player in NHL history to lead the league in scoring during a season in which he got traded. Thornton began the 2005–06 season with the Boston Bruins and finished it with the San Jose Sharks. Thornton finished the year with 125 points, edging out the New York Rangers' Jaromir Jagr (who had 123 points) to win the Art Ross Trophy.

CUP CHRONICLES

When Scott Niedermayer won the Stanley Cup for the first time with the New Jersey Devils in 1995, he brought the Cup to his hometown in Cranbrook, British Columbia and hiked with it up to the top of a mountain outside the city. In 2007, when Scott and his brother Rob won the Cup with the Anaheim Ducks, they flew it to the peak

of Bull Mountain in a helicopter and posed for pictures on the glacier at the top.

Scott and Rob Niedermayer hoisting the Cup on Bull Mountain

NAME GAME

In 1924 the Boston Bruins became the first American team in the NHL. Charles Adams, who owned the team, chose brown and yellow as the Boston colours because those were the same colours as the signs on the grocery stores he owned. Adams held a contest to name his hockey team. He had very definite ideas about what kind of name he wanted: the name had to relate to an untamed animal, and the animal had to be big, strong, ferocious and smart. And, of course, it wouldn't hurt if that animal happened to be brown. The name Bruins was the winner of the contest. "Bruin" is a word for bear that was used in old tales and fables. Today, Boston's colours are black and yellow.

DID YOU KNOW?

Because so many hockey players were serving in the Armed Forces during World War II, the NHL actually considered closing down before the start of the 1942–43 season. But both the Canadian and American governments asked the league to keep going. They felt that hockey was good for the morale of the soldiers overseas and for the people on the homefront.

NHL on Board

Professional athletes had been allowed to play hockey at the Winter Olympics since 1988, but the first time that the NHL truly got involved with the Olympics was at the 1998 Winter Games in Nagano, Japan. The NHL shut down its schedule for two weeks in February of 1998 so that its players could join their various national teams.

Olympic Gold and Stanley Silver

In 1980 defenseman Ken Morrow became the first player to win an Olympic gold medal and a Stanley Cup Championship in the same year. Morrow was a member of the American Olympic team that captured a surprising gold medal at Lake Placid that February. After the Olympics, Morrow joined the New York Islanders and won the Stanley Cup in May.

DID YOU KNOW?

When hockey made its first appearance at the Olympics, it was part of a spring sports festival held prior to the start of the 1920 Summer Olympics in Antwerp, Belgium. The Winnipeg Falcons represented Canada that year. They beat Czechoslovakia 15–0, the United States 2–0 and Sweden 12–1 to bring the gold medal home to Canada.

Women of Winter

Women's hockey made its first appearance at the Winter Olympics in Nagano, Japan in 1998. Before that, four official Women's World Championship tournaments had been held between 1990 and 1997. In every World tournament, Canada had beaten the United States in the final. The two countries met again in the gold medal game at the Olympics, but this time the United States won. Since then, Canadian women have bounced back to win Olympic gold in 2002 and 2006.

One of a Kind

Only one player in hockey history — Connie Broden — has won a gold medal at the World Championship and won the Stanley Cup in the same season. Broden won the 1958 World Championship with the Whitby Dunlops, who represented Canada that year. Just six weeks later,

Broden joined the Montreal Canadiens on their march to the Stanley Cup. Although Broden had been a star player with Whitby and was the top scorer at the World Championship tournament with 12 goals and seven assists in seven games, he saw very little action with the Canadiens. In fact, Broden only played in one of the five games against Boston in the Stanley Cup Finals that year. Still, it was enough to get his name engraved on the famous trophy.

Nowadays, a feat like Broden's is impossible. Since 1977, when active NHL players were allowed to compete at the World Championship, the event has always taken place during the Stanley Cup playoffs. That means only players whose NHL teams didn't make the playoffs (or get knocked out early) have a chance to play at the World Championship.

Hockey App-titude

Gillian Apps made her first appearance with the women's national team at the Women's World Championship in 2004 and went on to be one of the top scorers for Canada's Olympic women's hockey team in 2006. Apps attracted a lot of attention because she's part of a famous hockey family: her grandfather, Syl Apps, is a member of the Hockey Hall of Fame. He starred with the Toronto Maple Leafs in the 1930s and '40s and won the Stanley Cup three times. Gillian's father (Syl Apps Jr.) was a star player with the Pittsburgh Penguins in the 1970s.

DID YOU KNOW?

Four of the six Sutter brothers (Brian, Darryl, Duane and Brent) went on to become coaches in the NHL. In 1998–99, Brian Sutter became the first player in NHL history to win 300 games as a coach after scoring 300 goals as a player.

Born in the U.S.A.

The first American player to be selected first overall in the NHL Entry Draft was Brian Lawton in 1983. The Minnesota North Stars drafted him right out of high school. Lawton is also the first and only high school player ever to be chosen with the number one pick in the draft.

Twin Talents

Not only have there been many brothers who have played together in the NHL, but there have also been five sets of twins!

The first twins to play in the NHL were the two youngest of the six Sutter brothers who played in the league. Rich and Ron Sutter both broke into the NHL in 1982–83. Rich was with the Pittsburgh Penguins and Ron played for the Philadelphia Flyers. They faced each other in a game 17 times in their careers, but were also teammates for two seasons with the St. Louis Blues.

Patrik Sundstrom broke into the NHL with the Vancouver Canucks the same season that the Sutter twins made their NHL debuts. A year later, in 1983–84, Patrik's twin brother Peter joined the New York Rangers. The Sundstrom twins faced each other 18 times in their careers, but were also teammates briefly with the New Jersey Devils in 1989–90.

Twins Chris and Peter Ferraro saw limited action in the NHL between 1995 and 2002. They were teammates for most of their brief careers and never played in a game against each other. Neither have twins Daniel and Henrik Sedin, who have been teammates since they entered the NHL together with the Vancouver Canucks in 2000–01.

The NHL's most recent set of twins is Henrik and Joel Lundqvist. On December 14, 2006, Henrik was in net for the New York Rangers against the Dallas Stars. Playing centre for the Stars that night was a rookie who had just been called up from the minors — Henrik's twin, Joel. The Lundqvists became the third set of twins to play against each other in the NHL, but their meeting marked the first time that one twin was a goalie and the other was a forward.

Staal in the Family

After the Sutters, the next great hockey family may well be the Staal brothers of Thunder Bay, Ontario. As boys, Eric, Marc, Jordan and Jared Staal all played hockey together on a backyard rink built by their father.

Eric, the oldest of the Staal brothers, reached the NHL with the Carolina Hurricanes. The Hurricanes selected him with the second pick in the 2003 NHL Entry Draft, and he made it to the NHL right out of junior hockey in 2003–04. By 2005–06, Eric had become one of the top young stars in the game. During the season he ranked eighth in the NHL with 45 goals and 100 points. In the playoffs he led all scorers with 28 points in 26 games as Carolina won the Stanley Cup for the first time ever.

Shortly after Eric won the Stanley Cup in 2006, Jordan got drafted into the NHL. Just like Eric, he was picked second overall. Also like Eric, Jordan jumped to the NHL right away. He scored 29 goals as a rookie with the Pittsburgh Penguins in 2006–07.

Marc Staal is a year older than Jordan, but it took him a little longer to reach the NHL. The New York Rangers had selected him with the 12th pick in the 2005 NHL Entry Draft, but he didn't reach the NHL until the 2007–08 season.

Jared is the youngest of the Staal brothers. He played two seasons with the Sudbury Wolves of the Ontario Hockey League before being drafted by the Phoenix Coyotes in the second round of the 2008 NHL Entry Draft.

Malkin's Magic

When Evgeni Malkin joined the Pittsburgh Penguins in 2006–07, he set a modern rookie record by scoring a goal in each of his first six NHL games. Nobody else had begun his NHL career with such a scoring streak since the league's very first season of 1917–18!

BY THE NUMBERS

The record for the most goals by one team in a single NHL game is held by the Montreal Canadiens. On March 3, 1920, the Canadiens beat the Quebec Bulldogs 16–3. Here is a look at the highest-scoring games in NHL history.

Goals	Teams/Score
21	Montreal Canadiens 14, Toronto St. Patricks 7
	Edmonton Oilers 12, Chicago Blackhawks 9
20	Edmonton Oilers 12, Minnesota North Stars 8
	Toronto Maple Leafs 11, Edmonton Oilers 9
19	Montreal Wanderers 10, Toronto Arenas 9
	Montreal Canadiens 16, Quebec Bulldogs 3
	Montreal Canadiens 13, Hamilton Tigers 6
	Boston Bruins 10, New York Rangers 9
	Detroit Red Wings 10, Boston Bruins 9
	Vancouver Canucks 10, Minnesota North Stars 9

Date
January 10, 1920
December 11, 1985
January 4, 1984
January 8, 1986
December 19, 1917
March 3, 1920
February 26, 1921
March 4, 1944
March 16, 1944
October 7, 1983

DID YOU KNOW?

The NHL record for the most points by one player in a single game is 10! Darryl Sittler had six goals and four assists for the Toronto Maple Leafs on February 7, 1976. The Leafs beat the Boston Bruins 11–4 that night.

Darryl Sittler of the Toronto Maple Leafs

Son of Stastny

Paul Stastny was a rookie sensation with the Colorado Avalanche in 2006–07. In fact, he set an NHL rookie record by scoring a point in 20 straight games from February 3 to March 17, 2007. Overall, Stastny had 28 goals and 50 assists in his rookie season. His 78 points gave him the fourth-highest rookie total in Colorado franchise history. Who were the only franchise rookies to score more points than Paul Stastny? His father Peter Stastny and his uncles Anton and Marion back when the Avalanche were still the Quebec Nordiques!

Sidney Sittler?

Sidney Crosby has kind of an odd nickname — Darryl, as in Darryl Sittler. He earned it during his very first exhibition game with the Rimouski Oceanic in the Quebec Major Junior Hockey League. Crosby had four goals and four assists in that game. People started calling him Darryl after that because of Sittler's NHL scoring record.

Pucks versus Pitching

When Wayne Gretzky was a boy, he liked baseball even more than hockey. He pitched and played shortstop on local baseball teams while growing up in Brantford, Ontario. Gretzky was already such a great hockey player that newspaper reporters were interviewing him when he was only 10 years old. In his very first interview in 1971, Gretzky said he would like to be playing baseball with the Oakland A's and their star pitcher Vida Blue.

DID YOU KNOW?

The most goals ever scored against a team in an NHL game shutout is 15. The Detroit Red Wings beat the New York Rangers 15–0 on January 23, 1944.

Road Woes

Two teams in modern NHL history have gone an entire season with only one win on the road. Both were expansion teams in their very first season. The 1974–75 Washington Capitals were 1–39–0 on the road. The 1992–93 Ottawa Senators were 1–41–0.

BY THE NUMBERS

Longest Consecutive Goal-Scoring Streak

Games	Player, Team
16	Punch Broadbent, Ottawa Senators
14	Joe Malone, Montreal Canadiens
13	Newsy Lalonde, Montreal Canadiens
	Charlie Simmer, Los Angeles Kings
12	Cy Denneny, Ottawa Senators
	Dave Lumley, Edmonton Oilers
	Mario Lemieux, Pittsburgh Penguins

Longest Consecutive Assist Streak

Games	Player, Team
23	Wayne Gretzky, Los Angeles Kings
18	Adam Oates, Boston Bruins
17	Wayne Gretzky, Edmonton Oilers
	Paul Coffey, Edmonton Oilers
	Wayne Gretzky, Los Angeles Kings
16	Jaromir Jagr, Pittsburgh Penguins

Season

1921–22

1917–18

1920–21

1979–80

1917–18

1981–82

1992–93

Season

1990–91

1992–93

1983–84

1985–86

1989–90

2000–01

BY THE NUMBERS

Longest Consecutive Point Streak

Games	Player, Team
51	Wayne Gretzky, Edmonton Oilers
46	Mario Lemieux, Pittsburgh Penguins
39	Wayne Gretzky, Edmonton Oilers
30	Wayne Gretzky, Edmonton Oilers
	Mats Sundin, Quebec Nordiques

Season

1983–84

1989–90

1985–86

1982–83

1992–93

Wayne Gretzky with the Hart and Art Ross Trophies

Making History . . . Twice

On October 11, 2007, Mats Sundin became the top-scoring player in the history of the Toronto Maple Leafs. In fact, he broke the team scoring record twice in the same game! Well, sort of . . .

Sundin entered the game that night tied with Darryl Sittler for the all-time Leafs lead with 389 goals and 916 points. During the second period, Sundin was given credit for an assist on a Toronto goal. That gave him 917 points. The game was held up

Sundin saluting the crowd at the end of the game

for several minutes while the fans at the Air Canada Centre cheered. There was just one problem. Sundin knew that he hadn't actually touched the puck on the play. He didn't deserve the assist. Early in the third period, it was announced that the assist had been taken away. Sundin no longer had the record. But a few minutes later, he had it again. In fact, Sundin scored a goal this time, giving him 390 goals and 917 points to set new Leafs records in both categories.

NAME GAME

The Colorado Avalanche began in the World Hockey Association as the Quebec Nordiques. Nordiques is a French word that translates as "northmen." It was chosen because Quebec City was farther north than any other team in the WHA. In 1979 the Nordiques joined the NHL, but then moved from Quebec City to Denver for the 1995–96 season. They were renamed the Colorado Avalanche to symbolize the power of the Rocky Mountains. An earlier NHL team in Denver had been called the Colorado Rockies.

Starry, Starry (Starry) Night

On the night he broke the Maple Leafs scoring record, Mats Sundin was selected as the first, second and third star of the game. Many years before, on March 23, 1944, Montreal Canadiens legend Maurice "The Rocket" Richard had been named all three stars in a game against Toronto. Richard scored all five Montreal goals that night as the Canadiens beat the Maple Leafs 5–1.

CUP CHRONICLES

When New Jersey Devils goalie Martin Brodeur was a boy in Montreal, he and his friends used to play road hockey and pretend that they were playing for the Stanley Cup. So, when Brodeur won the Cup for the first time in 1995, he brought it home to

Montreal and got all his old buddies together for a road hockey game. The winners got to carry the Stanley Cup around in triumph! Brodeur's team lost the game that day, so when he won the Cup again in 2000, he organized a rematch. This time, his team won.

BY THE NUMBERS

The 1976–77 Montreal Canadiens still hold the NHL record of 132 points in a season, even though their mark of 60 wins is no longer the best. Here's a look at the NHL teams with the most wins and the ones with the most losses in one season.

Most Wins	Team/Season
62	Detroit Red Wings, 1995–96
60	Montreal Canadiens, 1976–77
59	Montreal Canadiens, 1977–78

Most Losses	Team/Season
71	San Jose Sharks, 1992–93
70	Ottawa Senators, 1992–93
67	Washington Capitals, 1974–85

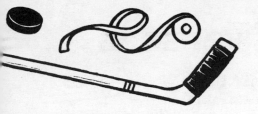 

Wins, Losses, Ties
(62–13–7, 131 points)
(60–8–12, 132 points)
(59–10–11, 129 points)

Wins, Losses, Ties
(11–71–2, 24 points)
(10–70–4, 24 points)
(8–67–5, 21 points)

NHL Overseas

The first regular-season NHL games to be played outside of North American were played in Japan. The Vancouver Canucks and the Anaheim Ducks opened the 1997–98 NHL season with a pair of games at Tokyo's Yoyogi Arena. One year later, the San Jose Sharks and Calgary Flames opened the 1998–99 season with two more games in the Japanese capital.

Ten years after their trip to Japan, the Ducks took part in the first NHL regular-season games to be played in Europe. The Ducks and the Los Angeles Kings opened the 2007–08 season with two games at the O2 Arena in London, England.

Oh, Brother!

Four sets of brothers once appeared on the ice in a single NHL game! It was a game between the New York Rangers and Chicago Black Hawks on

December 1, 1940. Lynn and Muzz Patrick and Neil and Mac Colville were teammates together on the Rangers. Max and Doug Bentley and Bob and Bill Carse all played for the Black Hawks.

Gentleman of Japan

On January 13, 2007, Yutaka Fukufuji became the first person born in Japan to play a game in the NHL. Fukufuji was a goalie with the Los Angeles Kings. He played the third period of a game that night against the Vancouver Canucks. Three nights later, Fukufuji got his first start against the Atlanta Thrashers. In all, he played four games for the Kings in 2006–07, but spent most of the season in the minor leagues.

Fukufuji was born in Tokyo on September 17, 1982, and played for the Kokudo Tokyo team in the Asian ice hockey league. He moved to North America in 2004 after being drafted by the Kings.

One, Two, Three

The 2006–07 season was the first time in NHL
history that players who finished first, second and
third in the scoring race had all once been first-
round NHL draft picks. Sidney Crosby — who won
the Art Ross Trophy that year — was the first pick
in 2005, Joe Thornton was first in 1997, and
Vincent Lecavalier was first in 1998.

Punch's Pretend Pick

In the 1974 NHL Entry Draft, Buffalo Sabres general manager Punch Imlach selected an imaginary Japanese player. Taro Tsujimoto was supposedly a centre with the Tokyo Katanas of the Japanese Hockey League. The Sabres selected him in the 11th round, 183rd overall. A few weeks later the NHL discovered that Tsujimoto didn't really exist. Imlach later admitted that he had played the prank because of his frustration over how long the draft was dragging on. Today NHL records list the 183rd selection of the 1974 Draft as an "invalid claim."

How Swede it Is

The first European-trained player to be chosen number-one overall in the NHL Entry Draft was Mats Sundin of Sweden. Sundin was picked first by the Quebec Nordiques in 1989.

DID YOU KNOW?

The NHL held its very first draft in 1963. Only 21 players were selected that year, but it wasn't the smallest draft in NHL history. Only 18 players were chosen at the 1967 draft, and just 11 players were picked in 1965.

Firsts from Russia

Ilya Kovalchuk became the first Russian to be selected first overall in the NHL Entry Draft when the Atlanta Thrashers picked him in 2001. Alex Ovechkin was the second player from Russia to go first overall when the Washington Capitals selected him with the top pick in 2004.

The Very First

The first player selected in the very first NHL Draft back in 1963 was Garry Monahan. The 16-year-old was picked by the Montreal Canadiens. It took him four years before he finally made his NHL debut. Monahan wound up only playing 14 games for Montreal, although he did go on to enjoy a 12-year career in the NHL.

NAME GAME

When Buffalo joined the NHL in 1970, team management held a contest to choose the name. They didn't want yet another team in the city to be named after buffaloes or bison. They wanted something fresh. They wanted something that hadn't been used by other teams before. They chose the name Sabres after a type of sword that was carried by military leaders.

It Was a Long One . . .

The 2000 NHL Entry Draft featured the most players ever picked in draft history. In all, 293 players were selected that year. The very last player picked in the longest draft ever was Lauri Kinos of Finland. Kinos never made it to the NHL.

DID YOU KNOW?

Only three goalies have ever been selected first overall in the NHL Entry Draft: Michel Plasse (Montreal Canadiens, 1968), Rick DiPietro (New York Islanders, 2000) and Marc-Andre Fleury (Pittsburgh, 2003).

NAME GAME

Before the team moved to Calgary in 1980, Atlanta's first NHL team had been known as the Flames. When the NHL returned to Atlanta, team owner Ted Turner chose the name Thrashers. He picked the name because the Brown Thrasher is the official bird of Georgia, and Atlanta is Georgia's capital city.

DID YOU KNOW?

The Memorial Cup is the championship trophy for junior hockey in Canada. The Ontario Hockey Association donated the Memorial Cup in 1919 in memory of the many Canadian hockey players who had been killed fighting in World War I.

CUP CHRONICLES

Doug McKay played just one game in his NHL career, but it was a pretty important one: it was during the 1950 Stanley Cup Finals for the Detroit Red Wings. McKay is the only player in history to play his only NHL game with a Cup-winning team during the Stanley Cup Finals.

Brothers versus Brothers

In the second round of the 2007 playoffs, Rob and Scott Niedermayer of the Anaheim Ducks played against Henrik and Daniel Sedin of the Vancouver Canucks. It was the first time since 1986 that each team in a playoff series featured a pair of brothers. Back then, Peter and Anton Stastny of the Quebec Nordiques played Dave and Wayne Babych of the Hartford Whalers.

NAME GAME

Los Angeles entered the NHL for the 1967–68 season. Original team owner Jack Kent Cooke chose the name Kings because he wanted to give his team an air of royalty.

Brothers in Arms

In 2007, Rob and Scott Niedermayer of the
Anaheim Ducks became the first brothers to appear
in the Stanley Cup Finals as teammates since Rich
and Ron Sutter with the Philadelphia Flyers in
1985. When the Ducks beat the Ottawa Senators to
win the Cup, the Niedermayers became the first
brother combination to win the Championship
since Brent and Duane Sutter with the New York
Islanders in 1983.

Brothers facing each other in the Stanley Cup
Final are even rarer than brothers being
teammates, but the Niedermayers have done that

too! Back in 2003, Scott was with the New Jersey Devils when they beat the Ducks. Before that, brothers had not faced each other in the battle for the Stanley Cup since Ken Reardon's Montreal Canadiens beat Terry Reardon's Boston Bruins way back in 1946.

Rare Pairs

In 2006–07, Pittsburgh Penguins star Sidney Crosby won the Art Ross Trophy with 120 points while Evgeni Malkin led all rookie scorers with 85 points. That marked the first time in 47 years that two players on the same team had led the league in scoring and in rookie scoring too. The last two teammates to accomplish the feat were Bobby Hull and Bill Hay of the Chicago Black Hawks in 1959–60.

DID YOU KNOW?

Odie Cleghorn, a star player in hockey's early days, is credited as being the first coach to change his lines "on the fly." Cleghorn coached the NHL's Pittsburgh Pirates from 1925 to 1929. Before Cleghorn's innovation, most coaches liked to play their top stars for as much of the game as possible. Even the coaches who did make line changes back then always made them after a whistle had stopped the play.

Big, Bad Bruins

Bobby Orr was just 18 years old when he joined the Boston Bruins in 1966. The following year, Phil Esposito was traded to the team. At that time, the Bruins had missed the playoffs for eight straight seasons and hadn't won the Stanley Cup since 1941. However, with Orr and "Espo" together, the Bruins were soon the best team in the league. Together, they won the Stanley Cup in 1970 and 1972.

In 1968–69, Phil Esposito became the first player in NHL history to reach 100 points in a single season. He won the Art Ross Trophy that year with 126 points. But, as good as Esposito was, there are many people who think that his teammate was the greatest player ever. Not only was Orr a brilliant defenseman, he was also one of hockey's best scorers. In fact, he is the only defenseman in NHL history to win the Art Ross Trophy. He led the league in scoring twice, first in 1969–70, and then again in 1974–75. Orr also scored the winning goal for Boston when they won the Cup in 1970. He won the Conn Smythe Trophy as the most valuable player in the playoffs that year, and also won it in 1972 when Boston won the Stanley Cup again.

The Broad Street Bullies

The Philadelphia Flyers were the roughest team in hockey during the 1970s. Because their home arena was on Broad Street in Philadelphia, local sportswriters dubbed the team "The Broad Street Bullies." Flyers fans would say their team was aggressive, but most other teams just thought they were dirty! Still, the Flyers were talented as well as tough. They won the Stanley Cup in 1974 and again in 1975. When the Anaheim Ducks won the Stanley Cup in 2007, they became the first team since the Flyers in 1975 to lead the league in penalty minutes and win the Stanley Cup in the same season.

BY THE NUMBERS

The record for goals in an NHL season has more than doubled since Joe Malone first set the standard with 44 in the league's first season. Here's how the record has grown over the years:

Goals	Player	Season
44	Joe Malone	1917–18
50	Maurice Richard	1944–45
50	Bernie Geoffrion	1960–61
50	Bobby Hull	1961–62
54	Bobby Hull	1965–66
58	Bobby Hull	1968–69
76	Phil Esposito	1970–71
92	Wayne Gretzky	1981–82

BY THE NUMBERS

Wayne Gretzky won the Art Ross Trophy as scoring champion more times than any other player in NHL history. Here is a list of players who have won the Art Ross Trophy the most times:

Player	Wins
Wayne Gretzky	10
Mario Lemieux	6
Gordie Howe	6
Jaromir Jagr	5
Phil Esposito	5
Stan Mikita	4

Comeback Kids

In the Stanley Cup Finals in 1942, the Toronto Maple Leafs fell behind the Detroit Red Wings three games to nothing. They rallied to win the next four in a row and won the Stanley Cup four games to three.

No other team in NHL history has ever come back to win the Stanley Cup after losing the first three games of the final series.

NAME GAME

The name for Minnesota's new NHL team was selected more than two years before it played its first game. On January 22, 1998, it was announced that the team would be called the Minnesota Wild. The name was chosen to reflect the natural, rugged wilderness of the area. It was also chosen because of the great enthusiasm of Minnesota hockey fans.

Glittering Goalies

Patrick Roy was the first goalie in NHL history to win 500 games in his career, doing it with a 2–0 win over the Dallas Stars on December 26, 2001. At the end of his career, Roy had tallied 551 wins; he had 289 with the Montreal Canadiens and 262 with the Colorado Avalanche, making him the only goalie in NHL history to win 200 or more games with two different teams.

On November 17, 2006, Roy got some company in the 500-win club: Martin Brodeur. While he was growing up in Montreal, Brodeur idolized Patrick Roy. Though Brodeur lost three games in a row before finally winning his 500th, he still got to the milestone faster than Roy had. Roy got his 500th win in his 933rd game, while Brodeur got his in his 900th game.

Luongo Time Coming

Roberto Luongo's teams had never made the playoffs during his first six seasons in the NHL. When he finally did make it with the Vancouver Canucks in 2006–07, it seemed like he was going to make up for all that lost time in a single night!

In his very first playoff game on April 11, 2007, Luongo faced more rubber than any goalie ever had before in his playoff debut. The Dallas Stars fired 76 shots at Luongo that night in a game that went into four overtime periods. Luongo made 72 saves as Vancouver won 5–4. Luongo was just one save short of the record for saves in a single playoff game, which was set by Kelly Hrudey when he played for the New York Islanders. On April 18, 1987, Hrudey made 73 saves as the Islanders beat the Washington Capitals 3–2 in another quadruple overtime game.

Long Time for Trophies

Paul Coffey won the Norris Trophy as the NHL's best defenseman two years in a row, in 1984–85 and 1985–86. He later won the Norris for a third time, but not until nine seasons later, in 1994–95. No one in NHL history had ever won a trophy again after such a lengthy time in between.

Joe Sakic also waited a long time for a trophy win. Though he'd been a top player throughout his career, the Colorado Avalanche star was in his 13th season when he was rewarded with the Hart Trophy as NHL MVP in 2000–01. No Hart winner in NHL history had played so long in the league before winning the trophy for the first time.

Overtime Overdue

For nearly 50 years, Maurice Richard held the career record for overtime goals in the playoffs. "The Rocket" won six games for the Montreal Canadiens in sudden death situations from 1946 to 1958. Even though teams today can play twice as many playoff games in a year as they did in Richard's time, it took until 2006 for his record to finally be beaten. Colorado Avalanche star Joe Sakic did it with his seventh career overtime goal on April 24, 2006.

Hard to Ruffle His Feathers!

Before Roberto Luongo played his first postseason game, Anaheim Ducks goalie Jean-Sebastien Giguere had faced the most shots ever in a playoff debut. Giguere stopped 63 of 64 shots to lead the Ducks past the Detroit Red Wings 2–1 in overtime on April 10, 2003.

Giguere's win for the Ducks that night began one of the most remarkable streaks in playoff history. He won six more games in overtime without a loss during the 2003 playoffs, then won two more overtime games during his next playoff appearance in 2006. By the time he was finally beaten in an overtime game in the first round of the 2007 playoffs, Giguere had set an NHL record by playing 197 minutes and 52 seconds of overtime hockey without allowing a goal. That's like going nearly 10 periods — or more than three full games — without allowing a goal, in hockey's most pressure-packed situation! Giguere certainly didn't let the end of his streak fluster him either. He bounced back to win four more overtime games during the rest of the 2007 playoffs to help lead the Ducks to their first Stanley Cup Championship.